COMBATTING SHAMING
and Toxic Communities™

COMBATTING
"SLUT"
SHAMING

SUSAN MEYER

ROSEN
PUBLISHING®
New York

Published in 2017 by The Rosen Publishing Group, Inc.
29 East 21st Street, New York, NY 10010

Copyright © 2017 by The Rosen Publishing Group, Inc.

First Edition

Library of Congress Cataloging-in-Publication Data

Names: Meyer, Susan, 1986- author.
Title: Combatting slut shaming / Susan Meyer.
Description: New York : Rosen Publishing, 2017. | Series: Combatting shaming and toxic communities | Audience: Grades 7-12. | Includes bibliographical references and index.
Identifiers: LCCN 2015047939 | ISBN 9781508171157 (library bound)
Subjects: LCSH: Shame--Juvenile literature. | Bullying--Prevention--Juvenile literature.
Classification: LCC BF575.S45 M49 2017 | DDC 302.34/3--dc23
LC record available at http://lccn.loc.gov/2015047939

Manufactured in China

CONTENTS

INTRODUCTION

In 2014, Stevie Little was a high school student in North Carolina. She was going about her day as she normally did when she began to hear some ugly rumors. According to the rumors, Stevie had made a sex tape with her boyfriend, who was now showing the video to everyone at school. In an interview with Women's eNews, Stevie explained that her boyfriend shared the video with his English class and it spread from there. Stevie had no idea a video like this even existed! Her boyfriend had actually sexually assaulted Stevie when she was drunk and taken a video, of which she was unaware. She told the school guidance counselor, who in turn told the police. Stevie's ex-boyfriend now faces charges for the assault.

However, the story doesn't end there. Stevie didn't just survive an assault; she also faced a huge backlash from her community. Friends and people she trusted all had opinions about the case, and many of these opinions were incredibly hurtful. People called her names, and not just to her face. People in Stevie's hometown took to social media—sites like Instagram, Twitter, and Facebook—and posted horrible things. They said that she had wanted the assault to happen and that she was a slut and a porn star. After all that she had already been through, Stevie says being revictimized by the community was almost as traumatic as the assault itself.

Signs like this one, carried by a participant at a SlutWalk event in New York City, rightly declare that no one has the right to touch you without your consent, regardless of what you're wearing.

What Stevie experienced and what thousands of teens—and especially teen girls—experience each year is called slut shaming. Slut shaming doesn't mean the victim is a slut. Rather, slut shaming is a type of bullying in which a woman is criticized for her real or presumed sexual activity. A woman can be shamed because she has had sex, because of the number of sexual partners she has had, because of the way she dresses, or even just because of rumors about her sexual activity. Using words like *whore*, *slut*, and *ho* regardless of whether they are used in a joking way are all examples of slut shaming.

All types of bullying are toxic, but slut shaming can have particularly nasty consequences. It supports a culture that tries to control women's choices. Calling women names like slut, telling women what they can't wear, or controlling how women can express their sexuality is a problematic part of this culture. All of these actions support the idea that women's sexuality can be possessed by others. This type of culture leads to higher rates of sexual assault. Some people will claim that a victim of sexual assault was "asking for it" because of the way she dressed or the number of previous sexual partners she has had. This is one of the ways that slut shaming can be incredibly dangerous and harmful. Additionally, victims of slut shaming can become depressed or even suicidal. Women who are slut shamed online face additional harm to their reputations. College admissions counselors and prospective employers can see what people have said about them and form opinions that can't be reversed.

If you have ever been called a slut or made to feel bad about your sexual choices or the way you present yourself, know that you are not alone. The majority of teen girls will experience slut shaming or some form of sexual harassment at some point in their lives. This doesn't make it okay. It is important that people take a stand against slut shaming. This resource will cover the history and background of this issue facing society today as well as some of the important people who are working to combat it.

CHAPTER ONE

A BRIEF HISTORY
OF SLUT SHAMING

It can be hard to turn on the television, go to a movie, or walk down the street without hearing the word *slut*. Comedians, talk show hosts, and people walking in the halls at school all use the word casually. But what does this word really mean? Ask anyone to define the word *slut* and you'll probably get many different answers. Merriam-Webster defines it as "a derogatory word for a woman with many casual sex partners."

However, the word has taken on many more subtle meanings in casual use in schools and in the media. A slut can now refer to any woman who does things differently and goes against what is considered normal feminine behavior. A woman can be called a slut for being aggressive. She can be called a slut for having too many male friends. She can be called a slut for dressing a certain way. She can be called a slut because she is considered too flirtatious. She can even be called a slut because she rejected a guy who asked her out. A woman can be called a slut if she has slept with a number of men casually or even if she has never

Young women face a double-edged sword when expressing their sexuality. They are expected to act "sexy" and be appealing to men, but at the same time, they are chastised for it.

kissed a boy. This can be confusing and frustrating to a young woman, especially because being called a slut has historically had very harsh implications. For example, by being labeled a slut, a woman is also being labeled impure and unclean.

WHAT'S IN A WORD?

The word *slut* didn't always mean what it does today. The earliest appearance of the word is in Geoffrey Chaucer's *The Canterbury Tales*, written in the fourteenth century. Chaucer used the adjective "sluttish" to describe a man who was messy in appearance. In the fifteenth century, the word evolved as a label for women, but it still referred to untidiness and unkemptness and had nothing to do with a woman's sexual activity. Through the centuries the word was used to describe everything from a bad house-keeper to a piece of cloth dipped in fat and used as a candle. It is hard to say when exactly the slang term came to its current meaning, but linguists believe it was in the early twentieth century. Even today, the meaning and connotation of the word continues to grow and change. Some women even want to reclaim the word *slut* and use it as an empowering word.

The Shame Game

Slut is a slippery word that can take on many meanings. So what does slut shaming really mean? Shame is a powerful emotion. We've all done things we regret or that we wish we could take back. Bullies seek to take advantage of shame and use it as a weakness. They try to bring a victim's shame into the public light and mock him or her. This makes the bully feel stronger by making his or her target feel weaker. In cases of slut shaming, the victim might not have felt any shame before she was attacked. She might not have regretted her actions because she didn't feel she was doing anything wrong. The slut shamer seeks to force feelings of regret and humiliation onto her.

In an article for the website Thought Catalog, Laura, now twenty, describes going to a party with friends. She was dancing with her friends and trying to make them laugh by dancing in a silly way. She overheard two girls talking about her and saying she was slutty for dancing that way. Years later, Laura says she still thinks about that moment every time she dances. Another woman, Megan, describes a time when she was fifteen and excitedly shopping for cute dresses to wear to a party. When she came out of the dressing room, one friend said she looked like a slut. All her friends laughed, and Megan was very upset because she didn't think there was anything wrong with how she was dressed. Both Laura and Megan were blindsided by slut shaming. They didn't feel like they were doing anything wrong until someone came along and succeeded in making them embarrassed about it.

Slut shaming can take many forms. Sometimes it is overt. The slut shamer uses words likes *slut, whore*, or *ho* to hurt the victim. Other times the attack may be more passive-aggressive.

The 2004 comedy *Mean Girls* demonstrates the very real problem of girl-on-girl crime when it comes to slut shaming. Both men and women are guilty of shaming others.

The shamer may ask "Are you really going to wear that?" or make general comments about things "slutty girls" wear or do.

Slut Shaming Through the Ages

Slut shaming happens every day. It is not always as obvious as someone bullying another person to her face. Sometime it takes the form of whispers behind someone's back, rumors that won't go away, or anonymous messages online. It also doesn't have to seem mean. Sometimes judgmental behavior from friends can come through even in a joke. It's not uncommon for friends to call each other names, but judgment coming from friends can be very hurtful.

Unfortunately, slut shaming is not a new concept. While it didn't have a name the way it does now, slut shaming has existed through the ages. Examples of slut shaming can be found throughout history and in literature. For many centuries, women have been valued for their purity. There has been a long-standing myth from the Middle Ages that women were sometimes made to wear chastity belts. These devices were designed to keep a woman from having sexual contact with anyone who was not her husband—the husband held the key. This did not happen in practice but the story was used allegorically. Additionally, in many places, women were bought and traded in marriage. In India, the amount of money a man paid for his new wife was called a bride price. Other cultures called it a dowry.

The value of a woman was in producing children for her husband and supporting the home. The value of a woman was greater if she was known to be a virgin. So important was virginity that some cultures even had tests to prove that a woman was a virgin on her wedding night. Many of these tests were completely inaccurate and included testing a woman's urine, measuring the circumference of her neck, or checking for blood on the sheets after the wedding night. The latter method followed from the belief that a woman would bleed the first time she had sex because a layer of tissue called the hymen would break. Truthfully, none of these tests had much accuracy behind them. Because a woman's hymen can be ruptured in many ways without her having had sex, there is no medical way to tell for sure if a woman is a virgin.

For much of history, women were considered inferior to men. Women were not allowed to vote in the United States until 1919.

This eighteenth-century painting is called *Purity of Heart*. The woman's purity is symbolized by the dove and lilacs she holds and the white dress she wears. Throughout history, women's purity has been held as an important virtue.

Even today, women are not equal to men. They make less money at the same jobs and face double standards that men do not face. For example, men who have multiple sex partners or who display a casual attitude toward sex are usually applauded. Women who behave in the same way are shamed for it.

You may be familiar with the words *misogyny* and *patriarchy*. *Misogyny* means prejudice or hatred toward women. *Patriarchy* means a society that is controlled by men. Both of these concepts play into slut shaming. People—both men and women— who shame women for their sexual choices are supporting a patriarchal society that seeks to keep women from acting out or behaving in ways that are not considered appropriate for women. Remember, a woman can be called a slut even if she's not sexually active. Slut shaming is far more about controlling women than it is about upholding a moral standard.

Slut Shaming in the Media

In addition to historical records, slut shaming can be seen in popular culture through the years. In the 1850 American novel *The Scarlet Letter* by Nathaniel Hawthorne, the main character, Hester Prynne, is slut shamed. Because she committed adultery (she cheated on her husband), she is forced to wear the letter *A* embroidered in red on her dress. People in her New England town shun her because of her actions. You may or may not agree with Hester Prynne's actions, but the idea of forcing a woman to publicly acknowledge her shame as a punishment is sadly one that was not left in the 1800s.

Flash forward over a century. In the 2014 season of the reality television show *The Bachelorette*, the star, Kaitlyn Bristowe, was bullied on social media after she chose to have sex with one of the

DRESS CODE DEBATE

School is a place with many rules. These rules are to keep students safe and to prioritize their learning experience. There is a debate going on about school dress codes for girls. Some believe that the enforcement of these dress codes is sometimes a form of slut shaming.

A group of middle school students in Illinois petitioned for the right to wear leggings to school, and students at a New Jersey high school protested a school ruling that strapless dresses were not appropriate at prom. In both cases, the school argued that revealing clothing worn by girls was a distraction to boys. The girls argued that they should not be held accountable for what boys do.

Another issue is more frequent dress code violations for young girls who develop early than for those who are less developed physically. In a *Time* interview, Lucy, a middle schooler from Illinois, describes a day when she and a friend were both wearing the same type of athletic shorts. She was reprimanded and her friend was not. The teacher said that because of her body type, the shorts were too revealing. While the dress codes themselves are not necessarily slut shaming, rules must be put in place so that they are enforced fairly and equally for everyone.

contestants on the show before it was "allowed." The backlash she faced showed that women are still not supposed to decide where and when they have sex. Another example of society policing a woman's sexual agency occurred in 2012 when Sandra

Hester Prynne, the heroine of Nathaniel Hawthorne's *The Scarlet Letter*, is publicly shamed by her Puritan town. She is forced to wear a red "A" on her dress as a symbol of her adultery.

Fluke, an attorney and women's rights activist, wanted to speak at a committee meeting to encourage the government to force health insurance companies to cover the cost of birth control. Conservative radio show host Rush Limbaugh called Fluke a "slut" and a "prostitute" for wanting women to be able to access affordable birth control options. Limbaugh later apologized to Fluke, saying his comments were meant to be humorous.

Suffice it to say, slut shaming has been a part of history for quite some time. However, it has taken on an uglier side in recent years, thanks to the Internet. No longer do peers mock the girl with the scarlet *A* in the town square. Now a picture, video, or comment can be posted online and spread like wildfire through a school and beyond with the click of a button. Moreover, these images stay online forever. Even if they are taken down, it's impossible to know who downloaded them before they were deleted. The Internet has ushered in a whole new era of slut shaming and one whose consequences are far greater than they ever were before.

CHAPTER TWO

WHY DO PEOPLE BULLY AND SHAME?

Why is slut shaming such an issue? Why do shamers shame? People who judge others do so for a number of reasons. Sometimes the desire to shame comes from the shamers' own insecurities or as a defense mechanism. When boys and men use the word *slut*, it is usually a derogatory term. It defines women as playthings and objects. The word seeks to take women down a peg. Remember that a slut can be any woman who doesn't behave the way women are "supposed" to behave. This can be threatening to men. Rejection can also be a reason why men choose to slut shame a woman. In a Thought Catalog article, Christine, now twenty-one, describes what happened to her: "Prom night, my junior year of high school. My then-boyfriend wanted us to have sex after the dance and I wasn't ready. He called me a slut in the limo ride home in front of all our friends." By calling her a slut, her boyfriend was trying to make her feel lesser because he felt hurt by the rejection.

Women may be slut shamed for very contradictory and confusing reasons. A man might brand a woman a slut for rejecting him or for not returning his physical affection.

Girl on Girl Crime

It is not just men and boys who are guilty of slut shaming girls. In fact, girls and women are often guilty of it themselves. Think of the earlier examples of Megan and Laura. Both were shamed by girls, and in one case by a girl who was considered a friend. In the 2004 film *Mean Girls*, Tina Fey's character tells a group of high school girls: "You all have got to stop calling each other sluts and whores. It just makes it okay for guys to call you sluts and whores." Unfortunately, women are far from innocent when it comes to slut shaming.

In some cases, women may slut shame other women because they feel threatened by a woman who seems more confident or sexually aggressive. In other cases, calling another woman a slut or spreading rumors about her might be a way for a woman to distract attention from herself. If she is calling another girl a slut, it makes it less likely that she will be called one. In this case, she is setting herself up as a "good girl" who is able to identify and shame "bad girls" who step out of line. A young girl or woman being labeled a slut is being told she is doing something wrong, that she is doing something atypical for her gender, and that she needs to get back in line. It also has the dual purpose of being a warning to other girls: step out of line and you too could be called a slut. This makes other women less likely to go to the aid of the person who is being bullied and also more likely to bully her themselves.

Young women live in a world where they are constantly having to make choices about how they will be perceived. Studies show that girls start being slut shamed as early as elementary school or middle school. At this young age, girls can be labeled sluts, whores, or bitches for seeming too aggressive, standing up to

Rejection is difficult to cope with at any age, but there are healthy ways to manage it without lashing out and trying to shame others.

boys, or expressing opinions. They can also gain these labels for wearing makeup, developing early, or pursuing boys. The labels at this age are less about who is sexually active and more about who is perceived to have more sexual knowledge. Young women can find that knowledge of sex and boys is a double-edged sword. Girls are expected to know about sex and not be prudes, but at the same time they shouldn't know too much, have sex with too many people, or enjoy it too much or they will risk being labeled a slut.

NOT JUST FUN AND GAMES

Video games can be fun. The makers of video games are often men; however, there are some women who have broken into the industry. In August 2014, a controversy that would become known as Gamergate rocked the video gamer community. The controversy centered around sexism in the industry and particularly around a targeted harassment campaign against two female game developers: Zoe Quinn and Brianna Wu.

Gamergate began when an ex-boyfriend of Quinn's posted on his blog about her saying, among other things, that she had used her sexuality to get ahead in the industry. Soon many other men were commenting and calling Quinn a slut. Quinn (along with those who defended her) had her address and personal information released online (an action called doxing) and had people threaten to rape and kill her. Gamergate shows how scary words on the Internet can be. It also shows how slut shaming can be used as a systematic tool by men to take down women who they feel have stepped out of line. Men who don't want women involved in video game making use these threatening tactics to make that happen.

The Hierarchy of Slut Shaming

Slut shaming can also have interesting connections to hierarchy, or social class. In an article published in *Social Psychology Quarterly*, one researcher presents the results of a study on how women in colleges use the word *slut*. Researchers interviewed women living in dorms at the University of Michigan–Ann Arbor and the University of California–Merced about issues and attitudes toward sexuality, friendship, and partying. They followed up with the women over the course of five years.

Slut shaming can be a way of isolating someone from a group. It is one of many types of bullying that sends the message "you are different than I am."

The study determined that the word was often used not as a comment on a person's attitude toward sex or promiscuity but as a way of saying "you're different from me." Women who had more money used the word to describe women of lower social classes as "skanky" and "trashy." These higher status women used slut shaming as a weapon to differentiate women whom they considered beneath them. Women who had less money or status used the word *slut* to describe people who were "snobby" or "cliquish." By defining women who were different from them as "slutty," the implication is that their own behavior was fine.

Ultimately, the most important thing to remember if you are slut shamed is that the fault does not lie with you. As we've discussed, a woman can be shamed regardless of her actions. If you are a woman or girl, it might not be possible to conform enough that you will never be slut shamed. However, you can change the way you respond to it.

THE DANGER
OF WORDS

Bullying of all kinds is damaging. Slut shaming presents its own very harmful, and even dangerous, consequences. First of all, photos or messages about a woman posted online can follow her forever. They can influence relationships with friends and family. They can also keep her from being hired or accepted into colleges. Hurtful photos and rumors can become part of her digital footprint and follow her anytime anyone searches her name online. Even if the rumors are false, they can still follow her online forever.

Slut shaming can have other less obvious consequences also. Studies show that the fear of slut shaming can lead young women to be more likely to have unprotected sex. Young women don't want to be seen acquiring birth control. This is in part because of situations like what happened with Rush Limbaugh and Sandra Fluke, as discussed earlier. In that incident, Fluke was called a slut for even discussing women's access to affordable birth control options. Incidentally, a 2014 study by the Washington University

Rumors spread about a woman online can have serious consequences when she is applying to jobs and entering the workforce.

School of Medicine found that providing a woman birth control did not increase the number of sexual partners she had. That said, the stigma remains that by seeking birth control a woman is sexually active or planning to become sexually active, which makes her potentially open to slut shaming. A lack of access to and education about birth control increases the rate of teen pregnancy. If young women are shamed for asking questions about birth control and safe sex, they are more likely to practice unsafe sex.

Slut Shaming and Rape Culture

Another extremely damaging consequence of slut shaming is its connection with rape and sexual assault. When a woman is labeled a slut, she is assumed to be "easy," or that she will sleep with anyone. Men may feel that she is obligated to have sex with them. They may not even look for consent. Any time a woman is made to do anything sexual without her consent, it is an assault.

Even more troubling, a woman's sexual history is often used against her when trying her rapist in court. Police officers, lawyers, and the general public may say that a woman was "asking for it" because of the way she was dressed, the fact that she was drinking, or her previous number of consensual sexual partners. It cannot be stated too many times: a sexual assault is never the fault of the victim. Regardless of what she was wearing when she was assaulted or even if she had previously had consensual sex with the man who assaulted her. This is a phenomenon called rape culture. Rape culture is a theory first suggested in the 1970s. A "rape culture" is one in which women are blamed for their assaults, and attackers' actions are assumed to be normal.

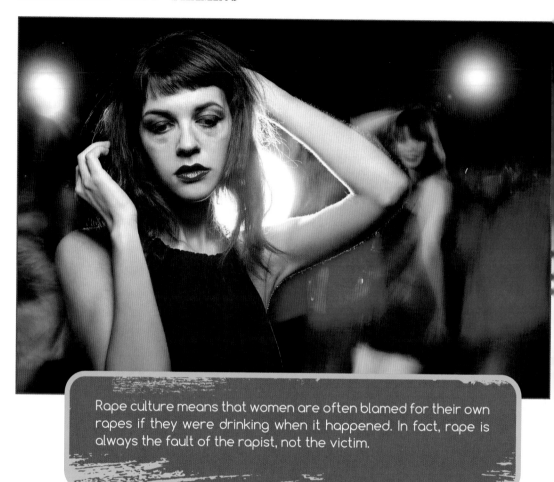

Rape culture means that women are often blamed for their own rapes if they were drinking when it happened. In fact, rape is always the fault of the rapist, not the victim.

In a rape culture, slut shaming can quickly turn into victim blaming. The following story may be difficult to read and involves an incident of sexual assault. In 2012 in Steubenville, Ohio, a sixteen-year-old girl passed out at a party from drinking. She was undressed, raped by several boys, and carried unconscious from party to party. The girl's assault was also recorded by the assailants on their phones. In these very disturbing videos, people can be heard laughing at her. She came forward and spoke out about her attack when photos and videos of it were spread around the school. Instead of getting sympathy, she received immediate backlash. Social media picked up the story and so did major newscasters. Some people said that they thought she was ruining the lives of her attackers by coming forward. Others blamed her for drinking in the first place and going to the party. Public opinion was telling her that she was guilty of causing her own rape because of her actions.

Rape and sexual assault is a huge issue. The US Bureau of Justice Statistics estimates that one out of every five women will be sexually assaulted during college. That is an astounding statistic. More startling still is the fact that among college age

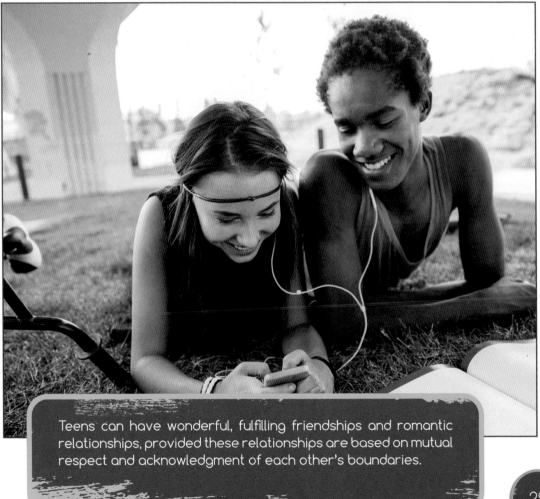

Teens can have wonderful, fulfilling friendships and romantic relationships, provided these relationships are based on mutual respect and acknowledgment of each other's boundaries.

women, nine out of ten will know their attacker. When we think of rape and sexual assault, we tend to imagine the danger of a man with a weapon snatching a victim in a dark alley. Some sexual assaults do happen that way; however, the numbers are increasingly showing that the majority of sexual assaults are not so straightforward. According to a study on sexual assault

THE CYCLE OF GENDER VIOLENCE

Some people say that slut shaming isn't a big deal. They think women shouldn't be so sensitive and should be able to take a joke. Calling someone a slut doesn't have lasting damage, they say, and words can't hurt.

None of these things is true. These smaller incidents of slut shaming and sexism are called microaggressions. Unlike a major traumatic event, they might not stick with you as long, but over time they build up and have lasting effects. Small incidents, such as calling women sluts and generally feeling it is okay to shame women, lead to larger and worse events such as trying to control a woman's choices, sexually harassing her, stalking her, or even assaulting her. In order to make big changes in a culture, sometimes you have to start at the smaller, seemingly less important actions to stop the bigger ones.

in colleges released by the National Institute of Justice, many women who were assaulted were under the influence of alcohol or drugs or otherwise incapacitated.

Some people say that the solution is to tell women not to drink or not to go to parties or not to wear certain clothing. These are all forms of slut shaming and ultimately not productive. A woman can do all manner of things to avoid being sexually assaulted, but the only one who is truly at fault is the one who chooses to victimize her. The only way to change these numbers is for the perpetrators themselves to be taught about consent. Part of this is to teach men to respect women and to not call them sluts or see them as sexual objects.

The Somber Truth About Slut Shaming

Not everyone is able to cope with the trauma of slut shaming. Some turn to drugs as a way of dealing with it. In her book *I Am Not a Slut*, Leora Tanenbaum describes the story of a woman she interviewed named Mia. Mia was a cheerleader and had developed early in middle school, which she believed is why she was targeted by slut shamers. At a party in seventh grade, she and some other girls were talking about who was or was not a virgin. Several girls said that they had had sex, so Mia said that she had too, even though she hadn't. She wanted to fit in, and she didn't want to feel left behind. A week later, news had spread all over the school that Mia wasn't a virgin. A girl started a petition saying that Mia was a slut and should die. Many students in the school signed the petition and were later punished by the school for it. Students blamed Mia for the punishment and began to lash out at her even more. Mia felt depressed and

Being slut shamed can have profound impacts on a young woman's emotional and mental well being. It can lead to feelings of isolation and depression.

helpless. She began smoking pot and later doing harder drugs. Throughout high school and college, she wore baggy clothes to try to hide her body. After being slut shamed relentlessly, she no longer felt comfortable in her own skin. She wanted to draw as little attention to herself as possible.

Mia's story illustrates several of the short- and long-term effects of slut shaming. When girls and women are told that they don't have ownership of their bodies or their choices about their bodies, they can grow insecure and withdrawn. Taking drugs can be a way of coping with this insecurity, but it is obviously a very damaging and unhealthy one. Other potentially unhealthy coping mechanisms include refusing to eat, avoiding all physical touch, and developing body image issues. Worst of all, some victims of slut shaming take their own lives.

The following story may be difficult to read, but it shows how dangerous and tragic the consequences of slut shaming can be. Rehtaeh Parsons was a fifteen-year-old straight-A student who loved science and playing with her sisters. In 2012, she went to a party near her home in Nova Scotia, Canada. At the party, Parsons was raped by four boys. One of the boys took a picture of her being assaulted and shared it around school. The photo soon went viral. Parsons was shunned at school. Her fellow students attacked her on social media and in person. Boys texted her asking to have sex with her, and girls texted to call her a slut. She left school, and she and her family moved so that she could get a fresh start elsewhere. Parsons sought help for depression and anger following the attack and was even hospitalized once. It was not enough. In 2013, Parsons took her own life. Both the original attack and the continued harassment were too traumatic.

Not all cases of slut shaming end as tragically as Parsons's story. However, Parsons's is sadly not the only story that ended this way. According to the Centers for Disease Control and Prevention, suicide is currently the second leading cause of death among young people twelve to twenty-four years of age. Research further indicates that the rate of suicide among teen girls specifically is rising at an alarming rate. It should be noted that slut shaming is just one factor of many that has led to this increase. That said, creating an environment in which teen girls are not put under such scrutiny, social pressure, and shaming would certainly improve the situation.

ADVICE FOR THE SHAMER AND THE SHAMED

Knowing how common slut shaming is and how damaging it can be, it can be easy to feel overwhelmed. However, there are many things that can be done by individuals to help stop slut shaming. It can begin with how you personally approach situations both in which you are the victim of shaming and in which you witness it happening to someone else.

If someone is spreading rumors about you or bullying you because of how you dress or how you express your sexuality, then tell a trusted adult, like a parent. If the bullying is happening at school, tell a teacher, principal, or guidance counselor. Part of the problem with slut shaming is that it aims to embarrass the victim, isolate her, and make her too ashamed to report the harassment. Remember that if someone calls you a slut or a whore, harasses you, or tells you that you should be ashamed of your choices, he or she is the one at fault. It can be hard to talk

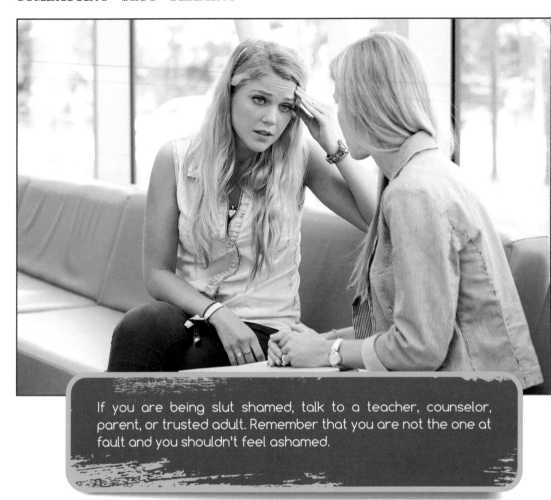

If you are being slut shamed, talk to a teacher, counselor, parent, or trusted adult. Remember that you are not the one at fault and you shouldn't feel ashamed.

to adults about personal—and especially sexual—details, but doing so can help make sure that the right people are punished.

If you feel comfortable and safe doing so, you can also confront the person who is slut shaming you. Explain to the slut shamer that he or she is slut shaming you and that you don't require his or her input and judgment on your personal choices. He or she might not listen to you and may fire back something just as hurtful, but it's possible you have planted a kernel of an idea that will still reach the slut shamer.

Bullying can feel particularly menacing when you are being harassed by a group. Try to leave the situation as soon as possible and find an adult.

If someone is harassing you online by commenting on your social media posts or sending you threatening messages, try blocking that person first. Before deleting the messages, save a record of them through screenshots so that you have proof of the harassment. This information can be useful later if you're sharing the harassment with an adult. If someone posts a photo of you or a disparaging message about you on his or her own social media, reach out to the site it was posted on to see if they will block the user or at least remove the offensive content,

CYBERSAFETY 101

Social media can be a fun way to share photos, videos, and messages with friends. However, it can also be dangerous to share too much. The key to protecting your identity and reputation online is to know who can see what you post. Here are a few basic guidelines to live by when posting online:

1. Know your privacy settings. Keep your profiles locked down to just friends you know in real life. And know that even then some people on your friends list might copy your photos or messages and share them with others. Don't post or share anything you would be upset to lose control of.

2. Think twice when sharing sexy photos even with your boyfriend. You may be in a trusting relationship now, but you never know how he'll react should the relationship end. Even if you send videos and images through sites like Snapchat that erase the images, you never know when someone will make a recording.

3. Never share photos or videos of anyone else without asking permission first.

4. Stay kind. This is a general rule of thumb for your interactions both online and offline. Don't post mean things on other people's pages. If everyone showed this same courtesy, the Internet would be a very different place.

especially if your real name was used. If you are a minor, you may have extra cause to get the site to take the content down.

While getting something removed from the Internet might seem like the hard part, moving past the emotional pain from the event can be even harder. This can be especially difficult if people in the school continue an ongoing campaign of harassment. In the previous chapter, we discussed some of the less healthy ways that people cope with trauma. If you are thinking about doing drugs or hurting yourself in some way, talk to an adult you trust right away. There are also hotlines you can call for immediate help, such as Teen Line (also available by chat at http://www .teenlineonline.org). You can also get free, confidential help twenty-four hours a day by texting "Go" to 741-741 to access the Crisis Text line (http://www.crisistextline.org).

Taking Control

One healthy way to cope with being slut shamed is to try to take control of the conversation. Slut shamers seek to take away control from their victims and make them feel guilty for their choices. It can be empowering to fight back and not stay silent. Rapper and model Amber Rose has spoken out about slut shaming. She said the first time she was slut shamed was when she was fourteen. The harassment continued throughout her life, including some very judgmental and hurtful remarks made by her ex-boyfriend Kanye West. Rose cried when giving a speech about her experiences but also said she was glad to be finally speaking out. She ended her speech with the following empowering words: "And even though I'm out here crying, I want to be the strong person that you guys can look up to." Rose found hope in telling her story and encouraging other women to free themselves from their own stories of slut shaming.

Rose is not the only celebrity to speak out about her experiences and demand change. In November 2015, the seventeen-year-old actress Ariel Winter, best known for her role on the television show *Modern Family*, posted a photo on Instagram. She was wearing a bikini and posing with her two nieces on a boat during a fun family outing. The photo received more than one thousand comments. Some of them were nice, but many of them told Winter that she should "put some clothes on" or that she was "asking for it." Instead of taking the photo down, Winter posted a message on her Instagram. This is part of that message:

> I typically never give power to the mean things people bravely say behind their computer screens on the Internet, but this is for the girls who are constantly bullied whether it be online or at school. You are not asking for anything because of what you are wearing- you are expressing yourself and don't you ever think you deserve the negativity as the consequence to what you are wearing- YOU ARE BEAUTIFUL.

You don't have to be a celebrity to take control of the conversation. You can be part of the solution by educating others. The first step is to make sure you are not part of the problem. One of the most important things you can do to help combat slut shaming is to not slut shame anyone yourself. A good place to start is to not use words like *slut*, *whore*, or *ho* even when joking around with friends.

Ariel Winter, an actress on the hit TV show *Modern Family*, has been outspoken about the grave problem of slut shaming. Correcting offensive behavior can effect change.

This can be easier said than done. Practice awareness. Be conscious of when you or others are speaking in a judgmental way about a woman's choices. If an actress is photographed in a magazine wearing a see-through dress, do you make a snap judgment? If a girl in your history class is always flirting with boys, do you resent her? If a friend sends you a video of a girl drunk and dancing on a table at a party, do you pass it on? Think about why you feel a certain way about these women. Consider the fact that their choices don't affect yours. If you take the time to think through each interaction and process your feelings about it, you

Bullying often feeds on a mob mentality. Don't be afraid to speak out against the group and defend someone who is being bullied. Remember that you may be a target one day.

might start to find it easier to resist slut shaming. You can delete the video and encourage the friend who showed it to you not to pass it on. You can avoid making a comment on the celebrity's character even if you choose to say you don't personally care for her dress. Undoing years of cultural bias can take some time. Don't be upset if you find these thoughts creeping in from time to time as you work to build your own awareness. You can also use this skill to help spread the message and teach awareness to others.

The second most important thing you can do is to call others out when they are slut shaming. If a friend points out a girl's short skirt or comments on rumors about her, remind him or her that neither affect who she is as a person. If you hear a bad rumor about someone in person or online, encourage people not to spread it. Depending on the situation, you might also report it to an adult. If everyone focused on policing his or her own choices and didn't try to shame others for theirs, the world would certainly be an easier place to live.

Starting a conversation about slut shaming can be incredibly difficult. If a friend says something mean about someone else, the easiest thing to do is laugh along. Instead of doing that, try to encourage your friends to think about why they are being judgmental. Ask them the same questions you asked yourself. Approach the situation in a friendly way. You might end up having a valuable conversation that could help inspire change. Helping one person to see things differently can ultimately cause a bigger change than you realize. In addition to thinking about his or her own actions, that person may go on to inspire great change in others, too!

CHAPTER FIVE

BREAKING THE
CYCLE OF SHAME

Slut shaming is a part of our culture. As long as people think it's okay to judge women for their choices and to try to bring them down for not behaving a certain way, slut shaming will happen. The only way to stop the shame is to break the cycle. This means allowing women to make their own choices, regardless of whether or not they are the choices you personally would make. In the previous chapter, we considered some ways that you can help make a difference at your school by just starting a conversation. In this chapter, we'll look at ways some people have taken that conversation even further. Many people aren't happy with slut shaming and are making big changes to help combat it.

Starting the Conversation

There is a movement to stop slut shaming that includes podcasts, documentaries, organizations, and websites. In addition to trying to build awareness about the issue, the movement also seeks to help those who were victims of slut shaming to cope with the consequences without shame. Social media and the Internet have made bullying and spreading rumors faster and more powerful than ever, but they have also improved communication and activism. People can share their stories online and gather in a community. This can help them realize they're not alone, and that they're not to blame. If shaming someone is an attempt to isolate her, the Internet helps keep that from happening. Even if you live in a small town, and it feels like everyone in your school has turned against you, you can still go online and search for stories about women who were slut shamed and have gone on to do great things.

Members of the movement against slut shaming have brought out the message in a number of different mediums. One way they've raised awareness is through the arts. A stage production called *SLUT: The Play* was developed by Katie Cappiello, Meg McInerney, and the members of The Arts Effect All-Girl Theater Company. It addresses the issues of slut shaming and rape culture by talking about the real-life experiences of teen girls in New York, New Jersey, Connecticut, and Pennsylvania. The play follows the story of Joanna, a girl who is assaulted while out in New York City with friends. The following is from the official synopsis of the play: "In a culture where silence, judgment, and over-sexualization allow sexual violence to thrive, will Joey find support and justice?" The play is performed in schools and venues around the country and encourages people to host events in their own schools.

In addition to the play, the creators of *SLUT* also provide other resources to help students start campaigns in their schools. They call this the StopSlut Coalition. According to their official site, StopSlut is "a worldwide, awareness-raising activist network for young people of all genders." They are further committed

Kate Cappiello *(left)* and Meg McInerney, seen here at the New York Fringe Festival premiere, are the creators behind *SLUT: The Play*.

to "transforming rape culture into CARE (Communication, Accountability, Respect, and Empathy) culture by igniting positive attitudes toward sexuality through creative, student-driven plans of action." They provide activism starter kits including discussion guides, writing prompts, and meeting guidelines to help anyone start a StopSlut Coalition chapter in their school or youth group. If you're not sure where to start in creating change in your school, they provide the resources to get you going.

Can a Bad Word Go Good?

Some people think a solution to the problem of slut shaming is to reclaim the word *slut*. Reclaiming a word means changing its meaning. It can mean taking a word that has negative or degrading implications and making the word empowering.

One example of trying to reclaim the word *slut* is through the SlutWalk movement. SlutWalks are events held in major cities around the world in protest of rape culture and violence against women. In particular, SlutWalks emphasize that women's dress should not matter if they are assaulted. The first SlutWalk was held in Toronto, Canada, in 2011. It was organized in response to a Toronto police officer saying that women shouldn't "dress like sluts" in order to prevent sexual assault.

Women take part in these protest marches by carrying signs and chanting. Some women also choose to dress in sexy clothes like short skirts and midriff-baring tops. The point of the march is that they are happy to be called sluts because *slut* doesn't have to be a negative word. However, they reject the idea that by being sluts they, or any woman, ever deserves to be victimized. Basically, the SlutWalk movement says that

SlutWalk is a worldwide grassroots movement designed to challenge rape culture. Participants in these events believe it is possible to reclaim the world *slut* and use it in an empowering way.

women can use the word *slut* on their terms and not as a weapon against them.

There is another camp of people who believe the word should be deleted from dictionaries. They think the word *slut* has become too ugly to take back. Their argument is that even if some people use the word in a positive way, other people will still be using it in an ugly way. This idea has some merit. After all, even laughing and joking with friends and calling each other these names can still have an undercurrent of judgment in it. It can be surprisingly hard to determine who is using the word

VIOLENCE WON'T BE SILENCED

Olivia Melville is an Australian woman in her early twenties who posted a racy lyric from the song "Only" by Nicky Minaj and Drake on her Tinder dating profile. A man took a screenshot of her profile and posted it on Facebook and suddenly Melville's profile was flooded with sexist—and sometimes violent—comments.

Melville called the police but didn't think their action was fast enough. She wanted to see change and for other women not to face violent threats for having their privacy violated. Melville and a dozen other women began a group called Violence Won't Be Silenced. This advocacy group works to combat online sexual harassment. They maintain a Facebook page for women to write about incidents of online harassment they've faced. Members of Violence Won't Be Silenced have also given interviews to the media as they try to raise awareness about this important issue.

in a good way and who is using the word in a bad way. What do you think? Should the word *slut* be reclaimed for feminist empowerment? Or is it better if it's a word we move on from and leave in the past?

As part of the Amber Rose SlutWalk in Los Angeles, participants were encouraged to write messages of acceptance on the "Wall of No Shame."

Slut shaming is an epidemic. Like all bullying, it's born from the desire of some people to feel stronger by making other people feel smaller and weaker. Slut shaming is particularly nasty because it feeds on our culture's harsh double standards for women. A woman should be allowed to make her own choices

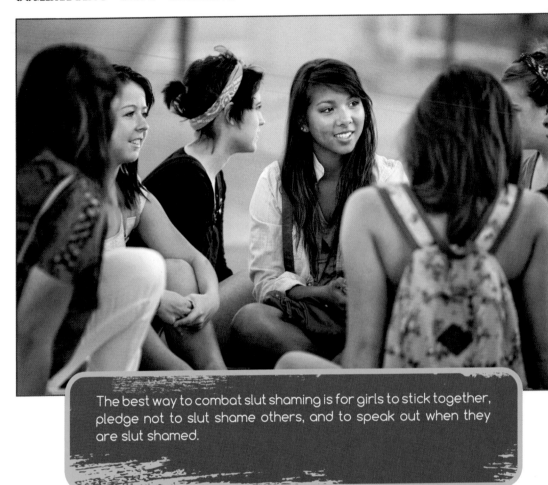

The best way to combat slut shaming is for girls to stick together, pledge not to slut shame others, and to speak out when they are slut shamed.

without being constantly pulled down. The sooner we forget about a feminine ideal, the sooner we can stop punishing women who break away from it in big ways or in small ones.

If you are being slut shamed, know that you are not alone and that you are also not at fault. Reach out to those around you for support. If you are witnessing other people slut shaming or being shamed, have the bravery to reach out to them. Encourage others to spread positive messages both online and face-to-face. If everyone works together, hopefully we will one day have a society where women can feel truly safe to be who they are.

ASSAILANT A person who attacks another person.

ASSAULT An attack.

CONFORM To try to be like everyone else.

CONSENT Giving permission, allowing something to happen.

DEFENSE MECHANISM A method of coping with or avoiding conflict.

DEGRADING Something that tears a person down.

DEROGATORY Insulting and hurtful.

DIGITAL FOOTPRINT All of the information about you that exists online.

HIERARCHY Organization in which people are ranked.

HYMEN A layer of tissue partially covering the opening of a woman's vagina.

MICROAGGRESSIONS Everyday interactions that communicate hostility.

PASSIVE AGGRESSIVE Subtly jabbing or attacking someone while avoiding a direct confrontation.

PATRIARCHY A cultural system that is run by men.

PERPETRATOR A person who commits a crime.

OVERT Obvious, clear.

RECLAIM To take back.

REPRIMAND To chastise.

RUPTURE To break apart.

SEXISM Discrimination based on gender.

TRAUMA An event too horrible to expect to face in daily life.

Canadian Women's Foundation
133 Richmond St. W., Suite 504
Toronto, ON, Canada M5H 2L3
416-365-1444
Website: http://www.canadianwomen.org
This organization helps women and girls in Canada and
    globally. One of their key tenets is that women should be
    free from violence, poverty, and rigid stereotypes that
    limit their potential.

Expect Respect
P.O. Box 19454
Austin, TX 78760
512-267-7233
Website: http://www.expectrespectaustin.org
Expect Respect engages youth, parents, schools, and
    community organizations in promoting healthy teen
    relationships and preventing dating abuse. Their goal is
    to mobilize youth leaders and create safe schools and
    communities.

Girls for a Change
P.O. Box 1436
San Jose, CA 95109
866-738-4422
Website: http://www.girlsforachange.org
Girls For a Change (GFAC) is a national organization that
    inspires girls to have the voice, ability, and problem

solving capacity to speak up, be decision makers, create visionary change, and realize their full potential. Through a number of programs, GFAC encourages girls, especially those in low-income areas, to inspire a positive change in their communities.

Girl Talk
3490 Piedmont Road NE, Suite 1104
Atlanta, GA 30305
Website: http://www.mygirltalk.org
Girl Talk is an international nonprofit peer-to-peer mentoring program that pairs high school girls with middle school girls to help them deal with the issues they face during their early teen years. The goal is to help young teenage girls build self-esteem and develop leadership skills.

Kid's Help Phone
1-800-668-6868
Website: http://www.kidshelpphone.ca/Teens/Home.aspx
Provided free and twenty-four hours a day for Canadians under the age of twenty, Kid's Help Phone provides resources and anonymous, confidential, and nonjudgmental counseling. Teens can access the service by phone or online.

National Organization for Women
1100 H Street NW, Suite 300
Washington, DC 20005
202-628-8669
Website: http://now.org

The National Organization for Women (NOW) is a nonprofit devoted to equality for women. It focuses on a number of women's rights issues including pay equality, women's health and body image, and representation of women in the media.

No Bullying
8th Floor, Chamber of Commerce House
22 Great Victoria Street
Belfast, BT2 7BA, Ireland
Website: http://nobullying.com
No Bullying is an online forum aimed at educating, advising, counseling, and, most importantly, helping to stop bullying, in particular, cyberbullying. Their website includes resources for teens on all types of bullying including slut shaming.

SlutWalk Toronto
Website: http://www.slutwalktoronto.com
The original SlutWalk campaign, this volunteer-run organization began in 2011. They have helped create a worldwide movement against victim blaming, survivor shaming, and rape culture.

StopSlut
917-261-4813
Website: http://stopslut.org
StopSlut is a youth-driven movement arising from the response to *Slut: The Play*, from The Arts Effect, that helps combat slut shaming by providing concrete tools to help

communities and individuals change perspectives and practices when it comes to girls and sexuality.

Teen Line
P.O. Box 48750
Los Angeles, CA 90048
301-855-4673
Website: https://teenlineonline.org
Teen Line is a confidential telephone helpline for teenage callers who can speak to or text with trained crisis counselors. It is toll-free for anyone living in California. The service receives more than ten thousand calls, texts, and e-mails each year.

Websites

Because of the changing nature of Internet links, Rosen Publishing has developed an online list of websites related to the subject of this book. This site is updated regularly. Please use this link to access the list:

http://www.rosenlinks.com/CSTC/slut

FOR FURTHER READING

Blue, Violet. *The Smart Girl's Guide to Privacy: Practical Tips for Staying Safe Online*. San Francisco, CA: No Starch Press, Inc., 2015.

Fossey, Richard. *Student Dress Code and the First Amendment: Legal Challenges and Policy Issues*. Lanham, MD: Rowman and Littlefield Publishing, 2014.

Hemmen, Lucie. *The Teen Girl's Survival Guide: Ten Tips for Making Friends, Avoiding Drama, and Coping with Social Stress*. Oakland, CA: New Harbinger Publications, Inc., 2015.

Holyoke, Nancy. *A Smart Girl's Guide: Drama, Rumors & Secrets: Staying True to Yourself in Changing Times*. Middleton, WI: American Girl Publishing, 2015.

Kilpatrick, Haley. *The Drama Years: Real Girls Talk About Surviving Middle School—Bullies, Brands, Body Image, and More*. New York, NY: Simon & Schuster, Inc., 2012.

Kramer, Kyra Cornelius. *The Jezebel Effect: Why the Slut Shaming of Famous Queens Still Matters*. Bloomington, IN: Ash Wood Press, 2015.

Martocci, Laura. *Bullying: The Social Destruction of Self*. Philadelphia, PA: Temple University Press, 2015.

Mayrock, Aja. *The Survival Guide to Bullying: Written by a Teen*. New York, NY: Scholastic, 2015.

Roberts, Emily. Express Yourself: *A Teen Girl's Guide to Speaking Up and Being Who You Are*. Oakland, CA: New Harbinger Publications, Inc., 2015.

Schatz, Kate, and Miriam Klein Stahl. *Rad American Women A-Z: Rebels, Trailblazers, and Visionaries Who Shaped Our*

History…and Our Future! San Francisco, CA: City Lights Publishers, 2015.

Simmons, Rachel. *Odd Girl Out: The Hidden Culture of Aggression in Girls*, rev. ed. New York, NY: Houghton Mifflin Harcourt Publishing, 2011.

Winnett, Erainna. *Tween Talk: A Tween's Guide to Social Success*. New York, NY: Counseling with HEART, 2014.

BIBLIOGRAPHY

Dockterman, Eliana. "When Enforcing School Dress Codes Turns Into Slut Shaming." Time. March 25, 2014. Retrieved November 4, 2015 (http://time.com/36997/ when-enforcing-school-dress-codes-turns-into-slut-shaming).

Fitz-Gerald, Sean. "*Modern Family* Actress Ariel Winter Shuts Down Instagram-Shamers Who Wanted Her to Cover Up." The Cut, New York. November 16, 2015. Retrieved November 18, 2015 (http://nymag.com/thecut/2015/11/ ariel-winter-instagram-shamers.html#).

GirlTalkHQ. "THE SLUT DIARIES: How Teen Girls Deal With Slut Shaming & Sexual Harassment." April 21, 2014. Retrieved November 8, 2015 (http://girltalkhq.com/ the-slut-diaries-what-teen-girls-think-of-slut-shaming-sexual-harassment).

Kutner, Jenny. "This Woman Received Rape Threats for Quoting Drake on Tinder." Mic. August 31, 2015. Retrieved November 1, 2015 (http://mic.com/ articles/124646/olivia-melville-was-slut-shamed-and-received-rape-threats-for-quoting-drake-on-her-tinder-profile#.Xy99rrtXo).

Lutz, Jamie. "7 Things You Might Not Think Are Slut-Shaming That Actually Are." Bustle. September 1, 2015. Retrieved November 1, 2015 (http://www.bustle.com/ articles/112849-7-things-you-might-not-think-are-slut-shaming-that-actually-are).

Mather, Katie. "15 Women Describe Their Most Traumatic Slut-Shaming Experience (So Far)." Thought Catalog. July

16, 2015. Retrieved November 1, 2015 (http://
thoughtcatalog.com/
katie-mather/2015/07/15-women-describe-their-most-
memorable-slut-shaming-experience).

Miller, Sarah. "The Link Between Slut-Shaming, Bullying, &
Femininity." Gender & Society. June 16, 2014. Retrieved
November 1, 2015 (https://gendersociety.wordpress.
com/2014/06/16/
the-link-between-slut-shaming-bullying-and-femininity).

Svazlian, Monique. "Slut Shaming Is Still a Thing: How
Women Are Shifting the Conversation Through the Arts."
The Huffington Post . February 9, 2015. Retrieved
November 1, 2015 (http://www.huffingtonpost.com/
monique-svazlian-cpcc-acc/how-women-are-shifting-the-
conversation-through-the-arts_b_6281368.html).

Tanenbaum, Leora. *I Am Not a Slut: Slut-Shaming in the Age
of the Internet*. New York, NY: HarperCollins, 2015.

Young, Natalia. "Teens Seek Refuge from Sex-Shaming
Onslaught." 2015 Teen Voices at Women's ENews,
Women's enews.org. February 26, 2015. Retrieved
November 1, 2015 (http://womensenews.org/story/
mental-health/150225/
teen-voices-teens-seek-refuge-sex-shaming-onslaught).

INDEX

About the Author

Susan Meyer is the author of more than fifteen young adult books. She is committed to the cause of raising awareness about slut shaming and violence against women. She volunteers at Safe Place, an Austin-based organization that provides safety and healing for survivors of domestic violence and sexual assault. The organization also works to change attitudes and policies and improve awareness around these issues. Meyer lives in Austin, Texas, with her husband, Sam, and cat, Dinah.

Photo Credits